INDIAN POLITY

FOR BEGINNERS

VEDANT DAS

ISBN 978-1-63957-137-6

<u>INDIAN POLITY</u>

Indian Polity and Governance

for beginners

<u>By</u>

Vedant Das

Contents

Preface

Hi guys,

Am a young writer, i write books on Social Science.. And as someone has said it true "If you have knowledge, let others light their candles in it." So just following it i took a initiative to write books!!

First of all this book is not meant to be read for any kind of exam and as the title of the book says this book is to give people a basic idea of how the Indian Government works and some information about Indian Constitution.

Thank you!

Keep supporting me!!!!

Acknowledgements

<u>THIS BOOK IS NOT MEANT TO BE READ FOR ANY EXAM PURPOSE AS THIS BOOK IS JUST TO GIVE PEOPLE A BASIC IDEA OF INDIAN POLITY.</u>

Acknowledgement is the most beautiful page in any project's final pages. More than a formality, this appears to me the best opportunity to express my gratitude.

My list can never begin without you, dear GOD. I feel that a simple "Thank You" is not enough for you dear readers....

Special thanks to my haters who always helped me to bring out the best. "Thank You people very much; your honest opinions are most welcome. I really respect your opinions. I mean it".

Now I would like to end this list by thanking each and every esteemed reader of this book Thank You dear Reader, Thank You for thinking of Buying this book and giving it a read, Thank You for Supporting my hard work and idea. I expect that you enjoy reading this book and end up getting a crystal-clear idea of the basic structure of Indian Polity and would appreciate if they send me their honest opinions, feedback, suggestions, complains etc in my mail id given below and *<u>PLS DO LET ME KNOW IF I WENT WRONG SOMEWHERE</u>*.

Thank You for all the love and support. Just keep connected.

VEDANT DAS

E-mail: <u>dasvedant2006@gmail.com</u>

CHAPTER ONE

HISTORY OF INDIAN CONSTITUTION

The Constitution is the fundamental law of a country which reflects the basic structure of the political system under which its people are to be governed. It establishes main organs of the State – the legislature, the executive and the judiciary, defines their powers, demarcates their responsibilities and regulates their relationships with each other and with the people.

Constitution of India was made by a Constituent Assembly which was specially which was specially set up under Cabinet Mission Plan 16 May,1946 to frame the Constitution of free India. The Constituent Assembly met for the first time on 9 December,1946. It had 389 members and Dr. Rajendra Prasad was its president. Then on 13the December 1946 Objective Resolution was moved my Jawaharlal Nehru and was adopted on 22 January 1947. Objective Resolution laid down the basic principles and the ideas on which the Indian constitution has to be made by the assembly. it was the objective resolution that give institutional expression to the fundamental commitments that is equality sovereignty and liberty. After that different committees were created which made drafts for different topic. When all drafts were ready then BN Rao who was the constitutional adviser of the Constituent Assembly wrote the draft of the Indian Constitution combining the different drafts of the committees.

Then a drafting committee was set up on August 29, 1947. Dr BR Ambedkar was its chairman. He is also known as the Father of Indian Constitution. The other members were M/s N.Gopalaswami Ayyangar , Alladi Krishnaswami Ayyagar , K.M Munshi , Sayed Mohd. Saadulla, N. Madhava Rau , D.P Khaitan.

The constituent assembly took 2 years 11 months and 17 days to produce the Constitution. Nearly ?6.4 crore were spent in making the Constitution. The constituent assembly submitted its report on 21stFebruary 1948. The draft constitution was introduced in the constituent assembly on 5thNovember 1948. The final draft was ready by 26thNovember 1949 but it came into force on 26thJanuary 1950 cause on this day in 1929 Indian National Congress passed a resolution demanding Purna Swaraj from British Government in Lahore session. To coincide with this day the Constitution was enforced on this day and thus 26thJanuary became our REPUBLIC DAY.

DYK?

- Indian Constitution is Fully handwritten by calligrapher from Santiniketan named Prem Behari Narain Raizada.
- Indian Constitution is the worlds lengthiest Constitution and currently has 470 articles divided in 25 parts and has 12 schedules.

CHAPTER TWO

SOURCES OF INDIAN CONSTITUITION

<u>British Constitution –</u>

- Parliamentary government
- Rule of Law
- Legislative procedure
- Single Citizenship
- Cabinet system
- Prerogative writs
- Parliamentary privileges
- Bicameralism

<u>American Constitution –</u>

- Fundamental rights
- Independence of judiciary
- Judicial review
- Impeachment of the president
- Removal of Supreme Court and High Court judges
- Post of vice-president

<u>Australia Constitution –</u>

- Concurrent list
- Freedom of trade, commerce and intercourse
- Joint-sitting of the two Houses of Parliament

Canada Constitution –

- Federation with a strong Centre
- Vesting of residuary powers in the Centre
- Appointment of state governors by the Centre
- Advisory jurisdiction of the Supreme Court

Ireland Constitution –

- Directive Principles of State Policy
- Nomination of members to Rajya Sabha
- Method of election of the president

USSR Constitution –

- Fundamental duties
- Ideals of justice (social, economic and political) in the Preamble

South Africa Constitution –

- Procedure for amendment of Indian Constitution
- Election of members of Rajya Sabha

France Constitution –

- Republic
- Ideals of liberty, equality and fraternity in the Preamble

Germany (Weimar) Constitution –

- Suspension of Fundamental Rights during emergency

Japan Constitution –

- Procedure Established by law

CHAPTER THREE

PREAMBLE OF INDIAN CONSTITUITION

The preamble is an introduction to a constitution and tells the fundamental values of the Constitution and aims and objectives of the Constitution. <u>It is a Part of Indian Constitution.</u>

The idea of our preamble is borrowed from the Constitution of U.S.A

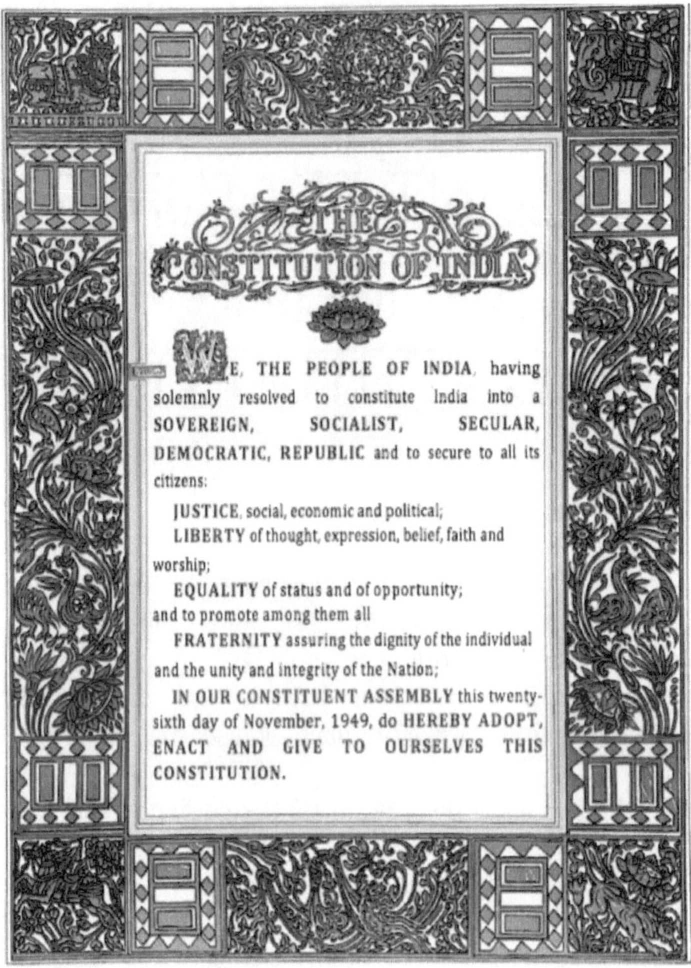

THE ABOVE PICTURE SHOWS THE PREAMBLE OF THE INDIAN CONSTITUTION

CHAPTER FOUR

SALIENT FEATURES OF INDIAN CONSTITUITION

<u>Most Exhaustive Constitution:</u>

Originally our constitution contained 395 article divided in 22 parts and 8 schedules. Right from the beginning our constitution is most comprehensive constitution in the world.

The British have no written constitution and Constitution of <u>USA had originally only 7 articles.</u>

- This 7 article Constitution of United States has been amended for 27 times up till now. The first 10 amendments are called Bill of Rights.

The constitution of Canada had 147 articles; Constitution of Australia had 128 articles.

Today, our constitution has grown more. <u>Now it has 470 articles divided into 25 parts and 12 schedules.</u>

- Please note that British constitution is not written. It is also called de facto or uncodified constitution.

But how an unwritten constitution would work?

- This is because, "unwritten" is a <u>misnomer.</u>The British constitution does not have document which can be called a "Constitution' but it is embodied in the written form, <u>within statutes, court judgments, and treaties</u>. Besides, parliamentary constitutional conventions and royal prerogatives are other written sources.

<u>Preamble:</u>

Indian Constitution has a preamble which gives an insight into the Philosophy of the Constitution.<u>It is a Part of Indian Constitution.</u>

- Initially the Preamble was not considered a part of the Constitution and its amendment was not accepted. In kesavanand Bharti v/s state of Kerala 1973 case the supreme court ruled that it is a part of the constitution and can be amended.

<u>Drawn from different sources:</u>

Our constitution has borrowed many things from many constitutions. Can we call is Plagiarism?

BR Ambedkar, The chairman of the Drafting Committee of the Constitutional Assembly said:

"As to the accusation that the Draft Constitution has [re]produced a good part of the provisions of the Government of India Act, 1935,"I make no apologies. There is nothing to be ashamed of in borrowing. It involves no plagiarism. Nobody holds any patent rights in the fundamental ideas of a Constitution...."

Yes, our constitution has borrowed good things from the Government of India Act 1935 and other contemporary constitutions of the world. The best provisions were selected from different sources and we should not be ashamed of that.

<u>Rigidity vs. Flexibility:</u>

Our constitution is rigid as well as flexible. While we shall study in the due course of time that Making Law is quite flexible and easy in comparison to amending a law. The amendment requires some more efforts. However, some parts can be amended with a simple majority while other can be amended by a special majority.

- Article 368 provides the procedure for amendment of the constitution.

<u>Sovereignty of the Country:</u>

The Preamble of the constitution declares that India is a sovereign state. It manages its internal and external affairs freely without any external forces.

- The policy of Nonalignment is a culmination of India's freedom in foreign policy.

<u>Democratic state:</u>

India is a democratic country where governing power is derived from the people by means of elected representatives of the people. The political authority is responsible to the people. This democracy is based upon the socioeconomic justice and equality of the opportunity.

- People can kick out the representatives who don't listen to them.

<u>Republic:</u>

India has adopted the "British" pattern of the parliamentary democracy.

- But India does not have a hereditary post of Head of the State. The Head of the state of President and he / she is elected.
- Indian President is indirectly elected by the people, because he is directly elected by the elected representatives.
- Any Indian without an discrimination to the caste / creed / religion can contest for Presidential elections and can occupy the office provided he fulfills the eligibility conditions as prescribed by the constitution.

The meaning of the Republic is that Head of the state is elected by the people. The head of the state is NOT a monarch in India.

Parliamentary Form of Government:

India has a parliamentary system of democracy. The council of ministers is responsible to the Lok Sabha here. The Council is Ministers is called Real executive. India has two types of executives. Real and nominal.

- President is the Nominal executive and Councils of Ministers is real executive,
- The council of Ministers is collectively responsible to the house of people. It means that they can remain in office so long as it enjoys the confidence of the house.
- Theoretically, parliament controls the functioning of the council of ministers , hence it is called parliamentary system

Socialist State:

Indian socialism is democratic socialism. The goals of the socialism are to be realized through democratic means.

- In the original constitution the term "Socialist" was not in the Preamble. It was added by the 42ndamendment in 1976.

Secular:

India is secular country. Here No religion is a state religion. The constitution provides equality treatment of al religions by the government and equal opportunities for all religions.

- The term "secular" was not in the Preamble. It was added by the 42ndamendment in 1976.

A blend of Federal and Unitary System:

The constitution of India establishes the country a partly federal and partly unitary government. There are separate governments in the Union and States and there is division of power. But, there are constitutional provisions and practices which have imparted unitary features by giving more powers to the centre. It provides Single Citizenship to all the citizens of the country, It has single constitution for both the centre and states.

- Jammu & Kashmir has a separate constitution

The parliament has power to legislate on the matters included in the state list. There are emergency provisions which make the system virtually a unitary system. The Change in the names and boundaries of the states can be done by the Parliament of India. There is an integral judiciary system. There are all India services such as IAS, IFS and IPS. The Governors of the states are agents of the President. There is an election commission which is central agency for elections at all levels. There is unequal representation of the states in council of States (Rajya Sabha), The Planned development of the whole country is responsibility of the planning Commission. The states are dependent on center for economic assistance and grants.

Integrated Judiciary:

In United states there are separate Judicial systems for the Union and the states. In India the Judiciary is integrated. The supreme judicial courts are not in states. The states have high courts but the verdicts of these courts are subject to appeal to the Supreme Court. The Constitution has made the High Court's subordinate to the Supreme Court.

Universal Franchise:

Our constitution provides adult and universal franchise to all citizens. Every citizen who is above 18 years has a Voting Right without any discrimination.

- 61stconstitutional amendment 1989 reduced the age of voting eligibility from 21 years to 18 years.
- Another term used for universal franchise is "common suffrage".
- France was the first country which provided Universal male suffrage in 1792, for the National Convention, enacted by law in 1793.

CHAPTER FIVE

CITIZENSHIP

Citizenship is discussed in Part 2 of the Indian Constitution (Article 5-11) and in Citizenship Act ,1955.

ARTICLE 5 – Citizenship by Domicile.

Qualification to get citizenship under ARTICLE 5 –

- Should have a domicile in India.

Any of the following –

- Born in India
- Any on his/her parents are born in India
- living in India for 5 years before 26.01.1950

ARTICLE 6 – Migrant from Pakistan

Article 6 divides migrants from Pakistan into 2 parts –

- People wo migrated before 19.07.1948
- People who migrated after 19.07.1948

NOTE : 19.07.1948 was chosen cause on that day Permit System was introduced in both Pakistan and India using which people could travel between the two countries.

<u>People wo migrated before 19.07.1948 –</u>
<u>Will be considered Indian Citizen on 26.01.1950 if –</u>

- He/she was born in India / Either of his/her parents were born in India / Any of his/her grandparents were born in India.
- He/she should reside in India since the date of migration.
- People wo migrated after 19.07.1948 –
- Will be considered Indian citizen on 26.01.1950 if –
- He/she was born in India / Either of his/her parents were born in India / Any of his/her grandparents were born in India.
- Returned to India under permit of resettlement
- Resided in India after remigration for atleast 6 months
- Submitted application for registration of citizenship to an officer
- Registered as citizen by such officer.

ARTICLE 7 – Citizenship of persons who migrated to Pakistan

<u>India -> Pakistan (after 1st march 1947) – Not an Indian citizen even if qualifies for citizenship under article 5 and 6</u>

<u>India -> Pakistan -> India (after 1st march 1947) – Will be considered an Indian citizen if –</u>

- He/she was born in India / Either of his/her parents were born in India / Any of his/her grandparents were born in India.
- He/she should reside in India since the date of migration.
- People wo migrated after 19.07.1948 –
- Will be considered Indian citizen on 26.01.1950 if –

- He/she was born in India / Either of his/her parents were born in India / Any of his/her grandparents were born in India.
- Returned to India under permit of resettlement
- Resided in India after remigration for atleast 6 months
- Submitted application for registration of citizenship to an officer
- Registered as citizen by such officer.

ARTICLE 8 – Citizenship of people of Indian Origin but living outside India (any country except Pakistan)
Will be considered Indian citizen on 26.01.1950 if –

- He/she was born in India / Either of his/her parents were born in India / Any of his/her grandparents were born in India.
- Registered as Indian citizen by diplomatic representative of India in that country.

ARTICLE 9 – Not deemed to be an Indian citizen.
If anyone on their will take citizenship of any foreign country before 26.01.1950 then they cannot demand Indian citizenship under Article 5 , Article 6 and Article 8.

ARTICLE 10 – Any person who acquires citizenship through Article 5/6/7/8 then citizenship will continue but will be subject to laws passed by Parliament.

ARTICLE 11 – Gives power to Parliament that after 26.01.1950 it can make laws on matters of citizenship.

<u>CITIZENSHIP ACT,1955 –</u>

<u>Acquisition –</u>

Citizenship by birth – Born in India
Anyone born in India will have Indian citizenship if both parents are Indian OR any one parent is Indian and

other isn't a illegal immigrant.

Citizenship by Descent – People born outside India can get Indian citizenship by descent.

Parents of such child has to register him as Indian citizen proving that their baby doesn't hold passport of any other country.

Citizenship by registration – People from specified category can become Indian citizen –

- People living in India for 7 years from the date of application.
- People of Indian origin but living outside India.
- A person married to Indian citizen and living in India for 7 years from the date of filing application.
- Minor children of Indian citizen.
- Person of full age and capacity living in any commonwealth country or Republic of Ireland.

Citizenship of Naturalisation– People of following qualification if file an application for citizenship then central govt can register them as citizen –

- Not part of country where Indians are prevented from becoming citizen of their country.
- Cancel any other citizenship.
- Should be residing in India for 12 months from date of application.
- Good character.
- Adequate knowledge of languages in 8th Schedule of Indian Constitution.
- After getting certificate of naturalisation their aim should be to reside in India.

Govt of India can wave of all of these qualifications or a particular qualification for people who have performed distinguished service in Science/Arts/Philosophy/Literature/Peace/Human Rights.

Citizenship by Incorporation of territory – If any foreign territory becomes part of India then Govt of India will specify that which people from that territory will be considered Indian citizen.

<u>Loss of Citizenship -</u>

Renunciation – Make a declaration that you are leaving Indian citizenship.

Termination– If any Indian citizen on their will acquire any other citizenship.

Deprivation– Compulsory termination by govt. if –

- You have acquired Indian citizenship by fraud/illegal method.
- Disloyal to GOI.
- Communicated/provided information to enemy country during war.
- Within 5 years of acquiring Indian citizenship if that person has got 2 years of jail.

CHAPTER SIX

FUNDAMENTAL RIGHTS

Fundamental Rights are those rights which are given to the people for their all-round development, dignity and political freedom. It's called Fundamental in the sense that any law of the legislature or any action of an executive will be declared null and void if it violates the Fundamental Rights of the citizens. Citizens also directly move the SC/HC for enforcement of their rights.

Fundamental Rights are covered in Part 3 of Indian Constitution which includes Article 12 – Article 35.

<u>FUNDAMENTAL RIGHTS IN INDIA: -</u>

- Right to Equality
- Right to Freedom
- Right Against Exploitation
- Right to Freedom of Religion
- Cultural and Educational Rights
- Right to Constitutional Remedies

<u>**NOTE:**Previously we had 7 Fundamental Rights but in 44thamendment in 1978 Right to Property was made a legal right under Article 300.</u>

All Fundamental Rights except Right to life and personal liberty can be suspended during an emergency.

CHAPTER SEVEN

FUNDAMENTAL DUTIES

Rights and Duties go together. Without duties their can, be no rights. But originally in our Constitution there was no mention of duties. But it was introduced in 42ndAmendment act and are included in Part IVA under Article 51A. Unlike Fundamental Right, Fundamental Duties are non-enforceable and its objective is to give a warning against anti-social activities and promote discipline and commitment and remind us of our duties as an Indian citizen.

<u>Currently there are 11 fundamental duties for the Indian citizens which are as follows: -</u>

- To abide by the Constitution and respect its ideals and institutions, the National Flag and the National Anthem;
- To cherish and follow the noble ideals which inspired our national struggle for freedom;
- To uphold and protect the sovereignty, unity and integrity of India;
- To defend the country and render national service when called upon to do so

- To promote harmony and the spirit of common brotherhood amongst all the people of India transcending religious, linguistic and regional or sectional diversities; to renounce practices derogatory to the dignity of women;
- To value and preserve the rich heritage of our composite culture;
- To protect and improve the natural environment including forests, lakes, rivers and wild life, and to have compassion for living creatures;
- To develop the scientific temper, humanism and the spirit of inquiry and reform;
- To safeguard public property and to abjure violence;
- To strive towards excellence in all spheres of individual and collective activity so that the nation constantly rises to higher levels of endeavour and achievement.
- To provide opportunities for education by the parent the guardian, to his child, or a ward between the age of 6-14 years as the case may be.

CHAPTER EIGHT

DIRECTIVE PRINCIPLES OF STATE POLICY(DPSP)

Unlike Fundamental rights which are a kind of negative rights which tell us what not to do to achieve justice DPSP are positive rights which tell us what to do in order to achieve justice. While Fundamental Rights are more concerned for political justice DPSP is more concerned towards economical and social justice. DPSP are non-justiciable however Article 37 tells DPSP is the basic source of governance and legislature has to follow DPSP for making laws.

The Constitution of India does not formally classify the Directive Principles of State Policy but for better understanding and on the basis of content and direction- they can be classified into three categories: Socialistic Principles, Gandhian Principles, and Liberal-Intellectual Principles.

- ***Socialistic Principles***

These principles contemplate the ideology of socialism and lay down the framework of a democratic socialist state. The concept envisages providing social and economic justice, so that state should achieve the optimum norms of welfare state. They direct the state through- **Article 38, Article 39, Article 39 A, Article 41, Article 42, Article 43, Article 43** A and **Article 47.**

* ***Gandhian Principles***

These principles reflect the programme of reconstruction enunciated by Gandhi during the national movement. In order to fulfil the dreams of Gandhi, some of his ideas were included in DPSP and they direct the state through- **Article 40, Article 43, Article 43 B, Article 46, Article 47** and **Article 48.**

* ***Liberal-Intellectual Principles***

These principles inclined towards the ideology of liberalism and they direct the state through- **Article 44, Article 45, Article 48, Article 48 A, Article 49, Article 50** and**Article 51.**

Four new Directive Principles were added in the 42nd**Amendment Act of 1976**to the original list. They are requiring the state:

1. **Added clause in**Article 39:To secure opportunities for healthy development of children

2. **Added clause in**Article 39 as Article 39A: To promote equal justice and to provide free legal aid to the poor

3. **Added clause in Article 43 as Article 43 A:**To take steps to secure the participation of workers in the

management of industries

    4. Added clause in Article48 as Article 48A: To protect and improve the environment and to safeguard forests and wildlife

CHAPTER NINE

PRESIDENT OF INDIA

Article 52-62 of the Indian Constitution deals with the President of India. President of India is the first citizen of India. Unlike president of India Indian President is just a nominal head, which means President exercises all its powers on advice of the Council of Ministers.

Election:

• Done by a system of proportional representation by means of single transferrable vote.

• The elected members of Lok Sabha, Rajya Sabha and the State legislative assemblies (not

councils), and elected members of the assemblies UTs of Delhi and Pondicherry

• Hence, nominated members do not participate

• Only SC has the jurisdiction in case the election of President is challenged. Acts done by

President before declaration of SC to disqualify her are not invalidated and continue to remain

in force

• The election of an individual to the President's post cannot be invalidated on the ground of

incomplete electoral college

• Value of vote of 1 MLA = (Population of state as per 1971 census) / (Total number of elected

MLAs) X (1/1000). UP has highest vote value per MLA and Sikkim has lowest.

• Value of 1 MP vote = Total value of all MLA votes of all states / Total number of elected

members of the parliament

• Electoral quota = [Total number of valid votes polled / (1+1) = (2)] +1

Qualifications:

• Citizen of India

• >35 years in age

• Qualified for elections to the Lok Sabha

• No office of profit in the Union government or any state government or local authority or any

public authority

Term:

• 5 years

• Resignation can be tendered to Vice President

• Can be re selected any number of times

• Removal only by impeachment

• Continues in office before next President takes over

Removal/Impeachment

• Removed only by process of impeachment or "violation of the constitution" — constitution

does not define this.

• Charges can be initiated by either House of the Parliament

• Charges should be signed by $1/4^{th}$ members of the House and 14 days' notice served to the

President

• After this, impeachment resolution can be passed by majority of the $2/3^{rd}$ of total membership

of the House, and goes to the next house.

- This house now investigates the charges, where President has right to appear and be
 represented
- If the other house passes the resolution by 2/3 rd of the total membership, the President stands
 impeached
- Note: nominated members of the Houses can participate in the impeachment and only Houses
 of Parliament participate in the process; the elected members of the legislative assemblies of
 the states and the UTs of Delhi and Pondicherry do not participate in the impeachment of the
 President though they participate in his election (both the elected and nominated members of
 Parliament can participate in impeachment of the President).

<u>Powers of the President:</u>

<u>Legislative Powers: -</u>

- Calls and closes the sessions of the Parliament.
- Can dissolve the Lok Sabha
- Nominates 2 Anglo-Indians for Lok Sabha and 12 Anglo-Indians for Rajya Sabha
- Can bring ordinance during emergency
- Any bill passed from both houses of the Parliament needs approval of President to become and Act and come into force.

<u>Executive Powers: -</u>

- Any work in the country is done by his/her name.
- Appoints PM of India.
- On advice of PM appoints the Council of ministers.

- Appoints Attorney General of India, Comptroller and Auditor General of India, Chief Election Commissioner of India , other Election Commissioners, UPSC members, members of Finance Commission, governor of states.

Judicial Powers: -

- Appoints CJI and judges of SC and HC.
- Can take advice from SC on legal matters though he/she is not bound to follow it.
- Can pardon a person convicted of any offence by court.

Diplomatic Powers: -

- Any international treaty or agreement are made on behalf of the President of India.
- Represents India in other nation through ambassadors/ high commissioners.

Financial Powers: -

- Has to present Union Budget in Parliament but can present it through someone else.
- Has access to Contingency Fund of India.
- Appoints Finance Commission in every 5 years.

Emergency Powers: -
o National Emergency - Article 352
o President's Rule - 356 and 365
o Financial Emergency – 360
Military powers: -

- Supreme commander of defence forces of India.
- Appoints army general, navy admiral and air force marshal
- Can declare and also stop war against a nation

CHAPTER TEN

VICE PRESIDENT OF INDIA

After President Vice President is the highest position in India.

Election:

Article 66 says Vice President shall be elected by electoral college consisting of only MP's.

Nominated members of the Parliament also vote in election of Vice President.

Qualifications:

- Citizen of India
- >35 years in age
- Qualified for elections to the Lok Sabha
- No office of profit in the Union government or any state government or local authority or any
  public authority

Removal:

- Can resign by writing in hand to the President of India.
- Can be removed by resolution passed by Rajya Sabha supported by majority and agreed by Lok Sabha.

Powers and Functions:

- Ex-officio chairman of Rajya Sabha.
- Acts as president If there is a vacancy due to death, resignation or impeachment or if president is not able to perform his/her duties due to illness , absence or any cause.

Note: Acts as president till date new president is elected and new president must be elected within 6 months.

PRIME MINISTER OF INDIA

Prime Minister is the executive head of India and head of GOI. Prime Minister is appointed by the president.

Prime Minister has a term of 5 years and President appoints the leader of the party or coalition which gets majority in Lok Sabha.

Powers and Functions: -

<u>Executive Powers: -</u>

- Head of Council of Ministers.
- Advices President on appointment of Council of Ministers.
- Can change/amend decision of any Council of Ministers.
- Can advice president for resignation of a Minister.

<u>Appointment Powers: -</u>

- Advices President on appointment of CoM , AGI , CAG , SGI , EC , RBI govt etc.

<u>Legislative Powers: -</u>

- Can recommend President to dissolve Lok Sabha and order re-election.
- If PM resigns then automatically Council of Ministers gets dissolved and have to resign.
- Can advice President to start/end a Parliamentary session.

<u>Foreign Policy Powers: -</u>

- Implements India's foreign policy by hosting meetings with foreign countries.

<u>Other Powers: -</u>

- PM is the head of NITI Aayog , NDC , Inter-state council , National Water Resource Council etc.
- During emergency PM becomes head of Disaster Management Council.

<u>Important Duties: -</u>

- Announces important policies
- Gives report of CM's work, foreign policy updates, Cabinet administration activity to the President from time to time.

<u>***Removal/Impeachment: -***</u>

- If the Lok Sabha passes a no confidence motion by simple majority then PM including CoM have to resign.
- A prime minister can also resign from office

CHAPTER TWELVE

UNION COUNCIL OF MINISTERS (CoM)

Council of Ministers is the official name given to the body that includes all ministers. President of India exercises all his/her powers on advice of CoM.

Council of Ministers get their power from Article 74 and Article 75 of the Indian Constitution.

Appointment: -

Council of Ministers are appointed by the President on advice of Prime Minister. A minister has can or cannot be an MP and in case if the minister isn't an MP then he/she has to get elected as a MP within 6 months of appointment as a minister.

Responsibility: -

The CoM has 2 types of responsibility namely: (a) Collective responsibility (b) Individual responsibility

- Collective Responsibility– The CoM including PM is answerable to the Lok Sabha for every decision they take cause if Lok Sabha passes a no-confidence motion with majority support against the govt then the PM including the CoM has to resign , Any decision taken in cabinet is not accepted until all the ministers supports it , If a Cabinet Minister disagree with a decision of GOI after cabinet meeting then he/she has to resign as a minister.

- <u>Individual Responsibility</u>– The CoM is answerable to the PM because they were appointed on advice of PM and can be removed on advice of PM.

Composition: -

- Cabinet Ministers
- Ministers of state
- Ministers of state with independent charge
- Deputy Ministers

Role and Authority: -

- CoM takes all important decisions.
- Highest authority is PM whose decision is final and who may not agree to the decision of a minister.
- Cabinet Ministers are head decision making authority of their respective ministry.

THE PARLIAMENT

The Union Legislature of India is known as Parliament/ Bhartiya Sansad. Article 79 states that there shall be a Parliament consisting of Lok Sabha, Rajya Sabha and President.

Indian Parliament is bicameral legislature.

Lok Sabha (House of People): -

The MP's of Lok Sabha are elected directly by the people through general elections and MP's of Lok Sabha exercise power on behalf of the people and take up their interests and make laws for them.

Term: -

Lok Sabha has a term of 5 years but can be dissolved earlier by the President on advice of the PM.

Qualifications: -

- Indian citizen.
- Should be 25-year-old or above.
- Shall not hold any office of profit under GOI/any state govt.
- Other qualifications as prescribed by Parliament.

Rajya Sabha (Council of States): -

MP's of Rajya Sabha are elected indirectly by the people. They are elected by electoral college consisting of MP's and MLA's of all states. They look after interest of the states, regions and federal units.

Term: -

Rajya Sabha has a term of 6 years with $1/3^{rd}$ of its members retiring every 2 year.

Qualifications: -

- Indian citizen.
- Should be 30-year-old or above.
- Parliamentary elector of that state.
- Other qualifications as prescribed by Parliament.

President: -

President isn't a member of any house but a bill passed by both houses need ascent of President to become an Act and come in force. President can ask to reconsider a bill but if the same bill is passed again then President has to give ascent to that bill.

Functions: -

The functions of the Parliament are mentioned in the Indian Constitution in Chapter II of Part V. The functions of the Parliament can be classified under several heads. They are discussed below:

Legislative Functions

- The Parliament legislates on all matters mentioned in the Union List and the Concurrent List.
- In the case of the Concurrent List, where the state legislatures and the Parliament have joint jurisdiction, the union law will prevail over the states unless the state law had received the earlier presidential assent.

However, the Parliament can any time, enact a law adding to, amending, varying or repealing a law made by a state legislature.

- The Parliament can also pass laws on items in the **State List**under the following circumstances:

  - If Emergency is in operation, or any state is placed under President's Rule the Parliament can enact laws on items in the State List as well.
  - As per **Article 249,** the Parliament can make laws on items in the State List if the Rajya Sabha passes a resolution by ⅔ majority of its members present and voting, that it is necessary for the Parliament to make laws on any item enumerated in the State List, in the national interest.
  - As per **Article 253,** it can pass laws on the State List items if it is required for the implementation of international agreements or treaties with foreign powers.
  - According to **Article 252,** if the legislatures of two or more states pass a resolution to the effect that it is desirable to have a parliamentary law on any item listed in the State List, the Parliament can make laws for those states.

Executive Functions (Control over the Executive)

In the parliamentary form of government, the executive is responsible to the legislature. Hence, the Parliament exercises control over the executive by several measures.

- By a **vote of no-confidence**, the Parliament can remove the Cabinet (executive) out of power. It can reject a budget proposal or any other bill brought by the Cabinet. A motion of no-confidence is passed to remove a government from office.

- The MPs (Members of Parliament) can ask questions to the ministers on their ommissions and commissions. Any lapses on the part of the government can be exposed in the Parliament.

- **Adjournment Motion**: Allowed only in the Lok Sabha, the chief objective of the adjournment motion is to draw the attention of the Parliament to any recent issue of urgent public interest. It is considered an extraordinary tool in Parliament as the normal business is affected.

- The Parliament appoints a **Committee on Ministerial Assurances**that sees whether the promises made by the ministers to the Parliament are fulfilled or not.

- **Censure Motion**: A censure motion is moved by the opposition party members in the House to strongly disapprove any policy of the government. It can be moved only in the Lok Sabha. Immediately after a censure motion is passed, the government has to seek the confidence of the House. Unlike in the case of the no-confidence motion, the Council of Ministers need not resign if the censure motion is passed.

- **Cut Motion:**A cut motion is used to oppose any demand in the financial bill brought by the government.

Financial Functions

Parliament is the ultimate authority when it comes to finances. The Executive cannot spend a single pie without parliamentary approval.

- The Union Budget prepared by the Cabinet is submitted for approval by the Parliament. All proposals to impose taxes should also be approved by the Parliament.

- There are two standing committees (Public Accounts Committee and Estimates Committee) of the Parliament to keep a check on how the executive spends the money granted to it by the legislature.

Amending Powers

The Parliament has the power to amend the Constitution of India. Both Houses of the Parliament have equal powers as far as amending the Constitution is concerned. Amendments will have to be passed in both the Lok Sabha and the Rajya Sabha for them to be effective.

Electoral Functions

The Parliament takes part in the election of the President and the Vice President. The electoral college that elects the President comprises of, among others, the elected members of both Houses. The President can be removed by a resolution passed by the Rajya Sabha agreed to by the Lok Sabha.

Judicial Functions

In case of breach of privilege by members of the House, the Parliament has punitive powers to punish them. A breach of privilege is when there is an infringement of any of the privileges enjoyed by the MPs.

- A privilege motion is moved by a member when he feels that a minister or any member has committed a breach of privilege of the House or one or more of its members by withholding facts of a case or by giving wrong or distorted facts. Read more on Privilege Motion.
- In the parliamentary system, legislative privileges are immune to judicial control.

- The power of the Parliament to punish its members is also generally not subject to judicial review.
- Other judicial functions of the Parliament include the power to impeach the President, the Vice President, the judges of the Supreme Court, High Courts, Auditor-General, etc.

Other powers/functions of the Parliament

- Issues of national and international importance are discussed in the Parliament. The opposition plays an important role in this regard and ensures that the country is aware of alternate viewpoints.
- A Parliament is sometimes talked of as a 'nation in miniature'.
- In a democracy, the Parliament plays the vital function of deliberating matters of importance before laws or resolutions are passed.
- The Parliament has the power to alter, decrease or increase the boundaries of states/UTs.
- The Parliament also functions as an organ of information. The ministers are bound to provide information in the Houses when demanded by the members.

Sessions of Parliament: -

- Budget Session – End of January to May
- Monsoon Session – July to August
- Winter Session – November to December
- Joint Session – Called by President if a bill passed by one house is rejected by other/amended bill is not accepted by other house/ one house doesn't take action on a bill

given to it for consideration 6 months ago.

NOTE:The timing of sessions can be changed according to the situation but the time between two sessions cannot be more than 6 months.

CHAPTER FOURTEEN

SUPREME COURT OF INDIA

The Supreme Court is the highest and final judicial authority in India. The Supreme court currently consists of 34 justice including CJI of India.

Appointment of a Judge: -

Appointed by President on advice of PM and in consultation with CJI of India and currently the collegium process if followed to choose a justice for appointment.

Term of a Justice of SC: -

A justice of SC holds their office until 65 years of age.

Qualifications: -

- Indian citizen
- 5 Years of experience as a HC judge _OR_ 10 years of experience as a HC advocate.

Impeachment of Justice of SC: -

A judge can only be removed after an impeachment motion is passed by both houses of the parliament with special majority from each house.

Jurisdiction: -

Original Jurisdiction: -

- Dispute between GOI and one/more states
- Dispute between one/two/more states
- Disputes regarding enforcement of Fundamental Rights

Appellate Jurisdiction: -

- SC can hear appeals against the judgements of High Courts.

Advisory Jurisdiction: -

- Can advice President on legal matters but President isn't bound to follow that advice.

Court of Record: -

- SC judgements are deemed to be evidentially proved and lower courts can give such judgements on such cases.

SC can also punish people for contempt with 6 months jail/₹2000 fine/both.

Judicial Review: -

- SC can declare any law made by Union or state or any action of executive invalid if it is against the Constitution.

Other Powers: -

- Interprets the Constitution
- Can review its own judgements
- Can issue writs for enforcement of Fundamental Rights

<u>Things out of Jurisdiction: -</u>

- Financial matters
- Interstate water disputes
- Treaty disputes
- Military cases
- Court martial cases

CHAPTER FIFTEEN

GOVERNOR OF STATES

Governor is the chief executive head of the state. Article 153 of the Indian Constitution says that there shall be a governor of a state. Same person can be appointed as a governor of two or more states.

Appointment: -

Governor of a state is appointed by the President of India.

Eligibility: -

Citizen of India

- >35 years in age

- Not a member of Parliament or state legislature and if a member then he/she is deemed to have been vacated on date of assuming charge as a governor.

- No office of profit in the Union government or any state government or local authority or any

  public authority

Removal of Governor: -

President in effect of central government has the power to remove governor of any state at any time even without giving any reasons for his removal

However, this power cannot be exercised in arbitrary manner. It is to be exercised in rare and exceptional circumstances for valid and compelling reasons

Powers and Functions: -

Executive Powers: -

- Any work in the state is done by his/her name.
- Appoints CM of the state.
- On advice of CM appoints the State Council of ministers.
- Appoints Advocate General, CM of the state and on advice of CM appoints the state council of ministers, members and chairperson of state public service commission , state chief election commissioner.

Legislative Powers: -

This power of Governor can be classified further in to 2 sub-groups i.e. wrt to bills and wrt legislature.

- **With Respect to Bills:**

When a bill other than money bill is presented before Governor for his assent, he either gives assent to the bill, with hold his assent to the bill, return the bill for reconsideration of houses, but if the bill is passed again by state legislature with or without amendments, he has to give his assent or reserve the bill for consideration of President.

However, the Governor also cannot send money bill back for reconsideration. This is because the money bill would usually be introduced with prior assent of Governor only. In case the money bill reserved for Presidents assent, the President has to state whether he is giving assent or withholding his assent.

- **<u>With Respect to Legislature:</u>**

He has the power to summon, prorogue the state legislature and can also dissolve the legislative assembly when it loses the confidence (art 176).
<u>Financial Powers: -</u>
- He lays before the legislature annual financial statement (state budget)
- Money bill can only be introduced in state legislature on his prior recommendation
- No demand for grant can be made except on his recommendation
- Money from contingency fund can be withdrawn after his recommendation for meeting the unforeseen expenditures
- He constitutes finance commission for every 5 years to review the financial situation of municipality and panchayats.
<u>Judicial Powers –</u>

- President consults the Governor of the concerned state while making appointment to the judges of State High Court.

<u>Pardoning powers-</u>
He has the below pardoning powers against any offences to which state power extends.

- Pardon- completely absolve the offender
- Reprieve- stay on execution of sentence

- Respite-awarding lesser punishment in some special circumstances
- Remission- reduction of sentence without changing the character
- Commutation-substitution of one form with other

<u>Discretionary Powers: -</u>

- Ordinance making power

CHIEF MINISTER OF STATE

Chief Minister is the head of the state government and is appointed by the Governor of the state. Governor appoints the leader of the party or coalition which got majority in state legislative assembly.

Powers and Functions: -

<u>Executive Powers: -</u>

- Advices governor to appoint the state Council of Minister.
- Chooses ministers for different ministries and can interchange them.
- CM can advice governor to dismiss a minister.
- If CM resigns then automatically the state council of minister gets dissolved.

<u>Legislative Powers: -</u>

- Advices governor to start/end a legislative assembly session.
- Declares government policies.

- Can advice governor to dissolve legislative assembly any time.

Appointment Powers: -

- Advices governor on appointment of Advocate General, state council of ministers, members and chairperson of state public service commission , state chief election commissioner.

Other Powers: -

- CM is chairman of state planning board.
- Political head of all services provided by state to its people.
- Member of inter state council and national development council.

Removal of CM: -

A governor can remove a CM if the latter has lost confidence of majority of the Legislative Assembly.

CHAPTER SEVENTEEN

STATE LEGISLATURE

Article 168 says that every state shall have a state legislature consisting of governor and one/two houses.

The upper house is called Legislative Assembly and lower house is called Legislative Council.

Legislative Assembly (Vidhan Sabha): -

It consists of members directly elected by the people. Number of members are decided on basis of state population and 1 Anglo Indian is nominated by the governor.

Qualifications: -

- Indian citizen
- 25 years old or more
- Shall not hold any office of profit under state or GOI
- Any other qualification as prescribed by Parliament of India

Term: -

- Legislative Assembly has a term of 5 years but can be dissolved earlier by the governor on advice of CM.
- Its term can also be extended by one year at a time by parliament during national emergency.

Legislative Council (Vidhan Parishad): -
It consists of members elected by different people which are as follows: -

- $1/3^{rd}$ members are elected by MLA's.
- $1/3^{rd}$ members are elected by local bodies.
- $1/12^{th}$ members are elected by secondary school teachers.
- $1/12^{th}$ members are elected by university graduates.
- $1/6^{th}$ members are nominated by the governor of the state.

This process of election of members of Legislative Council is not given in Constitution so the current process followed is given in Representation of People Act.

Creation/Abolition of Vidhan Parishad: -
Legislative Council/Vidhan Parishad is created or abolished by resolution passed by Legislative Assembly by a special majority requesting parliament to create/abolish Vidhan Parishad.

Functions: -
The functions of the states' Legislative Council are only advisory in nature. If any Bill is passed by the Legislative Assembly and sent to the Council, and the Council refuses to give its approval, then the Assembly has the right to reconsider it. The assembly may pass it with or without the amendments proposed by the Council, and again send it to the Council. When a bill approved by the Assembly is sent to the Council for the first time, it may retain it for three months, but in the case when it is sent for the second time and is kept in the Council for one month only, the bill is deemed as having been passed. This evidently demonstrates the Assembly's absolute superiority over the

LC. In the case of Money Bills, the State Assembly's powers are the same as those of the Lok Sabha. It is evident that the position of the Vidhan Parishad is haplessly weak. Even, in theory, it cannot be compared to the Rajya Sabha that, in spite of being the upper chamber of the Union Legislature, has some effective powers.

- All the LC can do is delay the passing of a money bill by 14 days, a non-money bill by 3 months or a non-money bill that is sent back to it with recommendations by 1 month.
- There is no provision in the Constitution for a joint sitting of the State Legislature. It is to be noted that while the Vidhan Sabha can override the Vidhan Parishad, the vice versa is never possible. A non-money bill that is passed by the Vidhan Parishad can be rejected by the Vidhan Sabha more than once.
- The LC members do not participate in the election of the President of the country. Apart from that, they do not have any meaningful role in any bill's rectification nor in a constitutional amendment. In practical terms, the Legislature of a State implies its Legislative Assembly which possesses the following major powers and functions:

  - It can create laws on any subject in the State List; it can also create laws on the Concurrent List provided the law does not contradict or conflict any law already made by the Parliament.
  - The Assembly asserts control over the Council of Ministers. Assembly members can question the ministers, move motions and resolutions, and also pass a vote of censure in order to dismiss the state

government. The government ministry is collectively accountable to the Legislative Assembly. If the ministry is defeated in the Assembly, it amounts to the passing of a no-confidence vote against the government.

- The assembly controls the State's finances. A money Bill can emerge from the Assembly and it is considered passed by the LC after a lapse of fourteen days after reference made to it by the Sabha. It could reject or pass the grants or reduce their amount indicating rejection or adoption of the budget and hence, implying victory or defeat of the State Government. Therefore, no tax can be levied or withdrawn without the consent of the Vidhan Sabha.

- The Assembly has constituent powers. With reference to Article 368, certain Bills of Constitutional amendment after being passed by the Parliament would be referred to the States for the process of ratification. In these cases, the Vidhan Sabha has a role to play. It should give its judgement by passing a resolution by a simple majority indicating approval or disapproval of the said Bill. There is a provision wherein the President shall refer to the state assembly of a state before he recommends the introduction of a bill which concerns with the alteration of the concerned state's boundary lines or its reorganisation in such a manner that its territory is increased or decreased.

Limitations of State Legislature: -

- Certain types of Bills cannot be moved in the State Legislature without the previous sanction of the

President of India

- Certain Bills passed by the State Legislature cannot become operative until they receive the President's assent after having been reserved for his consideration by the Governor;
- The Constitution empowers Parliament to frame laws on subjects included in the State List if the Council of States declares that it is necessary and expedient in the national interest that Parliament should Legislate on these subjects
- Parliament can exercise the power to make laws for the whole or any part of the territory of India with respect to any of the matters enumerated in the State List, while a Proclamation of emergency is in operation

The Legislative competence of Parliament can also extend to the subjects enumerated in the State List during the operation of a proclamation of the breakdown of the Constitutional machinery

HIGH COURTS

High Courts are the supreme judicial organ of a state.

Appointment of Chief Justice and other judges of High Courts: -

- Chief Justice of a High Court is appointed by the President after consultation with governor of that state and Chief Justice of India.
- Other judges are appointed by President after consultation with Chief Justice of that High Court and Chief Justice of India.

Qualifications: -

- Indian citizen
- Held a judicial office for 10 years OR Advocate of High Court for 10 years.

Tenure: -

- A high court judge retires at 62 years of age.

Impeachment: -

- A judge can only be removed after an impeachment motion is passed by both houses of the parliament with special majority from each house.

Jurisdictions: -
Original Jurisdiction:

- Matters of admiralty, will, marriage, divorce, company laws and contempt of court.
- Disputes relating to election of MP and MLA
- Disputes regarding revenue matters
- Disputes regarding enforcement of Fundamental Rights.
- Cases transferred from sub ordinate courts involving interpretation of the Constitution

Writ Jurisdiction:

- Can issue writ on any matter and also for the enforcement of Fundamental Rights.

Appellate Jurisdiction:

- Can hear appeals against judgements of sub ordinate courts.

Supervisory Jurisdiction:

- Supervises lower courts and tribunals coming under its territorial jurisdiction.

Court of Record:

- Judgements of HC can be used by lower courts to give justice on similar matters.

<u>Judicial Review:</u>

- HC can declare any law of the legislature/action of executive null and void if it is against the Constitution.

MISCELLANEOUS

WHAT ARE WRITS??

Writs are legal documentation passed by a court that orders someone to perform an act or stop performing an act.

Types of Writs:

Habeaus Corpus:

It is the most powerful and most used writ. It means "to have a body"

It can be used if a authority detains a person illegally then the person/family members can approach the HC/SC and HC/SC will use writ of Habeaus Corpus to free that person.

Mandamus:

It means "we command".

HC/SC can use thus writ to ask any public official to perform his public duties.

Certiorari:

It means "to be certified".

Using this writ SC/HC can ask lower courts to submit their record of judgements for review and if any judgement is illegal then it is quashed.

Prohibition:

It means "prevention"

Using this writ SC/HC can prevent lower courts from making a wrong/illegal judgement.

Quo Warranto:

It means "By what authority"

Using this writ SC/HC can ask any public officer that by ehat authority he is in that office.

Thak You So Much Readers

Hey Readers hope you enjoyed reading and I hope that If you have read this far then you have got a crystal-clear basic idea about Indian Polity.

I again repeat my words **THIS BOOK IS NOT MEANT TO BE READ FOR ANY EXAM PURPOSE AS THIS BOOK IS JUST TO GIVE PEOPLE A BASIC IDEA OF INDIAN POLITY.**

And guys please correct me if I went wrong somewhere and do give me the feedback and you can mail me for any query you have! And your honest opinions and ideas are always the most welcomed!!

And for the last time THANKS A TON dear reader!!

SECOND EDITION COMING SOON with much more knowledge and much for fun till then

STAY HEALTHY! STAY SAFE! STAY HAPPY! STAY TUNED!

My mail id: dasvedant2006@gmail.com

www.ingramcontent.com/pod-product-compliance
Lightning Source LLC
Chambersburg PA
CBHW031326250726
48656CB00005B/1991